Original title:
Painted Moths Among the Unicorn Damp

Author: Johan Kirsipuu
ISBN HARDBACK: 978-1-80563-154-5
ISBN PAPERBACK: 978-1-80564-675-4

Echoes of Serendipity in a Hidden World

In the hush of twilight's glow,
Whispers weave through branches low,
A dance of fate in shadows cast,
Where dreams and truths are tightly clasped.

The brook hums soft with tales untold,
Of playful sprites in woods of gold,
They twirl beneath the ancient trees,
Where laughter mingles with the breeze.

Each pebble turned reveals a spark,
A secret path through realms so dark,
With every step, a journey stirs,
As magic dwells in silent purrs.

The air, it thrums with promises bright,
In hidden nooks of mystic light,
Where serendipity streams like dew,
And every heartbeat whispers true.

So let the wonders guide your way,
In twilight's charm, let shadows play,
For in this world of hidden grace,
Echoes of joy find time and space.

Dreaming in Tints of Enchantment

Beneath the veil of starry nights,
In whispered dreams take gentle flights,
Colors swirl in shades of blue,
Enchantment blooms, so pure and true.

A canvas spread of twinkling skies,
Where every hue a tale implies,
In moonlit gardens, secrets blend,
As time unravels, twists, and bends.

Glimmers of hope, a lavender dawn,
Paints the world with wishes drawn,
While fairies laugh in floral glades,
And magic sparkles in cascades.

Each heartbeat syncs with nature's song,
In rhythms soft, where dreams belong,
Between the folds of night and day,
Reside the dreams that gently sway.

So close your eyes and breathe it in,
Let wonder's tide ignite within,
In the realm of dreams, we take our chance,
To sway in tints of sweet romance.

Luminous Spirits in Gossamer Hues

In twilight's grace, they softly gleam,
Whispers of dreams in a quiet stream.
Dancing through shadows, a soft embrace,
Gossamer threads weave a timeless space.

Hues of the night when stars confide,
Secrets unfurling with every stride.
Fluttering whispers, a beckoning call,
Luminous spirits enchanting us all.

Moonlit laughter drifts on cool air,
Fleeting moments, both precious and rare.
In the stillness, a flicker of grace,
Gossamer hues paint the night's face.

Veiled in mystery, they flit and swirl,
Around the forest, their magic unfurls.
With every heartbeat, a tale anew,
Luminous spirits in gossamer hues.

Chasing Silence Where Fairies Linger

In the hush of woods, where shadows blend,
Whispers of magic around each bend.
Chasing silence, with soft, careful tread,
Where fairies linger, imagination led.

Glimmers of laughter, a shimmer of light,
Echoes that dance through the cool, velvety night.
A tapestry woven with stars up high,
Dreams take flight, as the fairies sigh.

Under the canopy, secrets unfold,
Stories of wanderers, both timid and bold.
Chasing the silence, hearts beat as one,
In the embrace of the night, dreams begun.

Sprightly and merry, they flit 'round the glade,
In clandestine meetings, enchantments are made.
Chasing their laughter, we discover the song,
Where fairies linger, we too, belong.

Echoes of Color in the Fading Light

As day departs, a canvas unfolds,
With echoes of colors more vivid than gold.
Brushstrokes of lavender, orange, and green,
In the fading light, a magical scene.

The sun bows low, casting shadows that play,
Twinkling reflections of the close of the day.
Crimson and cobalt dance on the breeze,
Echoes of color, an artist's reprise.

Time slows its march in this twilight hour,
Nature's brush paints with undeniable power.
Moments like whispers, held in the air,
Echoes of color, beyond compare.

From dusk into night, they softly collide,
In velvet embraces where dreams coincide.
A kaleidoscope world in the evening's plight,
Echoes of color in the fading light.

Enigma of the Velvet Night

In the still of the night, where shadows creep,
Lies the enigma that dreams softly keep.
Whispers of wonder float through the dark,
Secrets entwined in a luminescent spark.

Stars shimmer bright in the sable sky,
Holding the dreams of those who dare fly.
Every heartbeat echoes the soft, sweet call,
Of mysteries woven to cradle us all.

With every breath, a tale to unfold,
The night wraps tightly, both gentle and bold.
Through veils of darkness, old stories ignite,
In the depths of the enigma of the night.

As night blooms fully and weaves its star thread,
Magic awakens where silence once tread.
In its embrace, the impossible gleams,
Enigma of velvet night lulls us to dreams.

Whispers of the Enchanted Wing

In a grove where secrets dance,
Softly rustle leaves, in trance.
A feathered tale, the twilight sings,
Of magic realms and gentle swings.

Moonlit paths of silver hue,
Parenthesized in night's deep blue.
The whispers weave their tender lore,
Of dreams once lost, now found once more.

Glimmers flicker on the breeze,
A tapestry that stirs with ease.
Each breath held close beneath the stars,
A serenade to distant cars.

In shadows' play, the stories shift,
With every sigh, a precious gift.
The heart's beat echoes through the night,
In every soul, a flickering light.

The enchanted wing shall lead the way,
Through winding paths where fairies play.
With every step, we rise and fall,
In wonder's grasp, we'll hear it call.

Chimeras in Twilight's Embrace

Underneath the velvet sky,
Chimeras dance with a wistful sigh.
In shadows where the dreamers meet,
They twirl and spin on nimble feet.

A tapestry of colors glows,
Where every heartbeat gently flows.
Twilight curtains draw us near,
To whispered tales of joy and fear.

Each creature born from starlit night,
Sparks of wonder, pure delight.
Fables told from ages past,
In every heart, these echoes last.

Secrets linger, softly spun,
In the twilight where dreams are run.
Through the dance of mystery's weave,
We find the magic we believe.

So let the chimeras lead us on,
Through realms where dusk meets break of dawn.
In twilight's arms, we're never lost,
For in our hearts, we pay the cost.

Luminous Shadows in the Glade

In a glade where silence sings,
Luminous shadows spread their wings.
Dancing light in fractured beams,
Threads of silver, woven dreams.

Beneath the boughs, the secrets hide,
Whispers drift on the summer tide.
Glade of wonders, pure and bright,
Guardians of the fallen light.

Every petal glows with grace,
In this enchanted, sacred place.
A symphony of nightingale's song,
In perfect harmony, we belong.

As moonbeams kiss the tranquil earth,
Awakening the dreams of birth.
In shadows' arms, the stories soar,
Luminous echoes forevermore.

Hold close the light that brightly shines,
In every heart, a guess aligns.
The glade shall keep our secrets safe,
Where shadows dance and dreams are brave.

Fluttering Fantasies Under Starlit Veils

Under starlit veils of soft embrace,
Fluttering fantasies find their place.
In the gentle hush of night's caress,
Magic lingers, a sweet finesse.

With every flicker, stories rise,
Capturing dreams in moonlit ties.
A whisper to the night's cool breath,
In fluttering forms, we escape death.

Each star a tale, bright and bold,
Of painted skies and hearts of gold.
With hope as our guiding light,
We sail on dreams, through endless night.

In realms where wishes twist and glide,
The fantasies dance in timeless stride.
Through silken threads of twilight's weft,
We find the dreams that fate has left.

So let us soar on wings of gleam,
Through every pulse of hope we dream.
At dawn's first blush, when shadows flee,
Our fluttering hearts forever free.

Dance of the Ethereal Fauna

In moonlit glades, the fauns do prance,
With shimmering coats, they twirl and dance.
Their laughter echoes, sweet and bright,
Beneath the stars, in the gentle night.

A breeze of magic stirs the air,
While fireflies flicker, light and rare.
In joyous rhythm, the night unfolds,
As tales of wonder linger, bold.

Each leap and bound, a story told,
In silver threads of dreams untold.
With grace they weave through ancient trees,
In harmony with night's soft breeze.

The world beneath their nimble feet,
A tapestry where dreams do meet.
In every gust, a whisper flows,
And wraps the night in soft repose.

With dawn's first light, their dance shall fade,
Yet in our hearts, the magic stayed.
For in that glen, where spirits soar,
The dance of fauns forevermore.

Shadows that Color the Unseen Path

Through tangled woods where shadows creep,
A hidden path, where secrets sleep.
The whispers call, both faint and shy,
As twilight weaves its mystic sigh.

Each leaf a tale, in whispers spun,
Of journeys past, and battles won.
The shadows stretch, they twist and twine,
To mark the way, where fate aligns.

With every step, the heartbeats quick,
A pulse of magic, a sacred trick.
As colors blend in dusky light,
The unseen path reveals its might.

In flickers bright, the fireflies dart,
Guiding weary souls with gentle art.
Through veils of gloom, their glow will guide,
As shadows laugh, their spirits abide.

So trust the shadowed road you tread,
For in its weave, your dreams are fed.
Embrace the dance of light and dark,
Across the path, let hope embark.

Aurora of Imagination in the Hidden Hollow

In the hidden hollow, colors spark,
Imagination blooms, a vibrant arc.
Brush strokes dance on the canvas bright,
Painting dreams in the soft twilight.

With whispers of wonder, thoughts take flight,
As stars ignite the velvety night.
A ribbon of magic, swirling free,
Unfolds the stories yet to be.

The brook hums softly, a tune divine,
While trees stand tall, in silent line.
Each leaf a portal, each flower a key,
To realms of wonders we yearn to see.

Fantasy reigns where shadows play,
In the glow of dusk, where thoughts display.
Colorful visions in the air,
Awake the dreams that linger there.

So linger long in this sacred space,
Where imagination holds its place.
In the hidden hollow, hearts will soar,
For within its depths, we dream of more.

Whispers of the Celestial Night

In the cradle of night, the stars align,
With whispers soft, they intertwine.
Each twinkle tells a tale so old,
Of journeys vast, and hearts so bold.

The moon, a lantern, glows with grace,
Illuminating dreams in this sacred space.
As constellations weave their lore,
We gather 'round, forevermore.

The cosmic ballet, a sight to behold,
Where wishes take wing, and hope unfolds.
Each sigh of the night, a promise made,
In the symphony of starlight's cascade.

With each heartbeat, the universe sways,
In sync with the dreams that softly blaze.
The night unveils its hidden charms,
In the cosmic dance, we find our arms.

So listen close to the celestial song,
In its soothing rhythm, we all belong.
For in the darkness, there's a spark of light,
A reminder that magic fills the night.

Evocative Hues Across Enchanted Lands

In forests deep, where shadows play,
The hues of magic start to sway.
Emerald glints through autumn's sigh,
As golden leaves begin to fly.

Rivers whisper secrets old,
Reflections dance in emerald gold.
Sunsets blush in crimson dreams,
While twilight weaves its silken schemes.

Mountains rise with snowy crowns,
Their peaks kissed by the morning browns.
Each stone a tale, each path a song,
In this enchanted realm, we belong.

The sky, a canvas brushed with light,
Stars awaken in velvet night.
Dreams take flight on sapphire wings,
In this world where wonder clings.

Through every hue, a story swells,
In magic's heart, where beauty dwells.
Let eyes behold and hearts believe,
In colors we can hardly weave.

Celestial Tapestries in Fable's Embrace

Beneath the arch of twilight's dome,
Fables weave a tapestry home.
With threads of silver, gold, and blue,
Old tales whisper the secrets true.

Constellations illuminate the skies,
Each star a story that softly flies.
In dreamy dances, shadows twirl,
As night unfurls its mystery swirl.

Waves of dawn in soft pastel,
Render magic where dreams dwell.
Each moment holds a sacred grace,
In the warm embrace of time and space.

Clouds like castles drift afar,
Guarding wishes, each a star.
In the embrace of tales retold,
Hearts ignite in flames of gold.

In fable's arms, we find our flight,
Bound by the glow of starlit night.
Together we shall dream and dare,
In this celestial tapestry rare.

Whimsical Varieties in the Foggy Vale

Mist descends with gentle grace,
Hiding secrets in its embrace.
Flowers bloom in colors rare,
In the vale, where dreams repair.

Beasts of lore tread soft and quiet,
In the fog, where shadows riot.
Crickets hum their cloaked refrain,
In the heart of this mystic train.

Winding paths that lead us near,
To wonders lost, yet crystal clear.
Each turn reveals a brand-new land,
A whimsical world at our command.

Fables live in every sigh,
As we weave our dreams to fly.
With laughter ringing clear and bright,
In the vale, we chase delight.

Through addled thoughts and playful haze,
We dance along in dreamlike ways.
The fog conceals what hearts may crave,
In this vale where memories wave.

Mysteries Wrapped in Chromatic Whirls

Colors swirl in a vivid dance,
Each shade a whisper, each glance a trance.
Riddles hide in the painted night,
Inviting dreams to take their flight.

In gardens where the wildflowers sway,
Golden rays chase the shadows away.
Petals shimmer with laughter and jest,
Wrapped in mysteries, they weave their quest.

Whirling hues of the evening sky,
Where memories linger and softly lie.
Each twilight breath evokes a spell,
A secret story that none can tell.

Dreamers wander through the painted haze,
In chromatic paths that twist and blaze.
With open hearts, we seek and find,
The mysteries that color the mind.

Beneath the arcs of a twinkling light,
We share secrets, both day and night.
In the dance of shades, we profoundly swirl,
Embracing wonder in a vibrant whirl.

Celestial Skins Beneath the Moonlight

In the hush of night, they glow,
Whispers of magic, soft and slow.
The stars weave tales, bright and bold,
As secrets of the night unfold.

Dance of shadows, silken grace,
Each flicker holds a hidden place.
With every shimmer, dreams ignite,
In celestial skins 'neath the moonlight.

Soft lullabies from heavens high,
Caress the world with a gentle sigh.
Through silver beams, the spirits glide,
In ethereal beauty, they abide.

Time melts softly, lost in the air,
In grace, they find their ancient prayer.
The moonlight bathes in tranquil streams,
Cradling hearts wrapped in starlit dreams.

As dawn awakens, paves the ground,
The celestial skins lose their sound.
Yet in the heart, their glow remains,
In moonlit nights, magic sustains.

Dreamscapes Where Color Meets Myth

In realms where colors breathe and play,
Myth dances lightly, night and day.
With strokes of wonder, dreams entwine,
A canvas vast, both yours and mine.

Clouds painted gold, the skies unfurl,
In vibrant swirls, visions whirl.
Each hue whispers of stories rare,
A tapestry woven with gentle care.

Through valleys deep and mountains high,
Legends echo, reaching the sky.
Each whisper beckons, tales to share,
In dreamscapes where magic fills the air.

The sun dips low, the dusk ignites,
A palette rich with soft delights.
In shadows cast by fading light,
Dreams emerge, embracing the night.

As dawn approaches, colors fade,
Yet in our hearts, the dreams are laid.
In every hue, a myth persists,
In dreamscapes bright, existence twists.

Velvety Charades in a Mythic Grove

In the grove where shadows blend,
Velvety charades begin and end.
Whispers dance on every breeze,
In secret tunes, the heart agrees.

Beneath the boughs, where silence sings,
The feel of magic, sweetly clings.
With every rustle, tales unfold,
In the warmth of the grove's embrace, bold.

Glimmers of light through leaves do peek,
In murmured secrets, spirits speak.
The twilight wraps them, soft and tight,
In mythic games kissed by the night.

Around the roots, the world submits,
As laughter echoes, shadows flit.
Each fleeting glance, a fleeting chance,
In the grove's spell, they weave and dance.

When dawn arrives, the tales take flight,
Velvety truths hide in plain sight.
The grove will keep its whispered lore,
In every heartbeat, forevermore.

Stripes of Light in the Ethereal Forest

In the forest where sunlight breaks,
Stripes of light weave through the flakes.
Each beam a thread of gold and dream,
In whispered woods, where wonders gleam.

Through boughs entwined, soft shadows sway,
With every rustle, the spirits play.
The echoing laughter, sweet and bright,
A symphony draped in pure delight.

Each step reveals a tale untold,
In colors vivid, rich and bold.
As pixies twirl in dappled glow,
The forest breathes, its secrets flow.

In quiet moments, hearts take flight,
Beneath the kiss of fading light.
The ethereal whispers, soft and low,
Guide every wandering soul that goes.

As twilight casts its shimm'ring lace,
The stripes of light begin to trace.
In dreams of twilight, magic sings,
In the forest, where enchantment clings.

Murmurs of Magic in the Gloom

In the depths where shadows weave,
Whispers dance in twilight's thread.
Ancient spells and secrets believe,
Beneath the stars, where stories spread.

Cascading whispers, soft and low,
Rustling leaves in the night's tender care.
Trees confide what they know,
To the moon's glow, secrets laid bare.

A flicker of light, a sudden spark,
Glances shared with time unturned.
Through the dark, a path will arc,
In quiet corners, all shall be learned.

Muffled laughter in the air,
Elixirs brewed with a gentle grace.
Every heart finding a pair,
In the twilight's comforting embrace.

So listen close, let silence hum,
For magic dwells in the shadows' play.
In the gloom where dreams may come,
Murmurs of the lost lead the way.

Ethereal Wanderers at the Dusk's Edge

On the cusp where day meets night,
Figures drift in fading light.
Feathers brushed with silver sheen,
Boundless souls where dreams convene.

Ethereal whispers weave a tale,
Of journeys taken, hearts set sail.
In their eyes, the skies unfold,
Stories written in shades of gold.

Through twilight's breath, they glide and sway,
Tracing paths where shadows play.
Each footstep a fleeting spark,
Creating constellations in the dark.

Gathered close in nature's choir,
Notes of longing, hope, and fire.
The edges blur where they descend,
In dusk's embrace, all barriers end.

So let them dance, the hidden few,
In dreams they share, a world anew.
For at dusk's edge, we find our vow,
To wander on, beneath the bough.

Cascade of Light from a Hidden World

From caverns deep, a light shall flow,
Shimmering softly, a radiant glow.
Whispers echo where few have tread,
In this hidden world, magic is spread.

Waterfalls gleam with secrets untold,
Cascades of light that dance and unfold.
Crystals sparkle in twilight's embrace,
Mirror the stars in their fragile grace.

Voices echo through emerald trees,
Carried gently upon the breeze.
In this realm where wonders ignite,
Every shadow unveils the light.

Silhouettes of creatures, watchful and wise,
Guardians draped in the night's disguise.
Each flicker of flame, a story begun,
In the heart where the rivers run.

So seek the light from the depths below,
Let your spirit take flight and flow.
For within the dark, the hidden glows,
A cascade of magic that endlessly grows.

The Lure of Vibrant Shadows

Shadows dance on the edge of day,
Whispering secrets, soft and a-sway.
Colors bleed in a twilight swirl,
Mysterious tales begin to unfurl.

In vibrant hues, they twist and twine,
Drawn by the night's enchanting line.
A silent summons to hearts that yearn,
For within the dark, their passions burn.

Figures flicker, phantoms play,
Enticing souls who dare to stray.
Each heartbeat beats in sync with the dark,
Illuminated dreams ignite a spark.

Beneath the moon, a canvas wide,
Every shadow holds a dream inside.
Casting light where the wild dreams soar,
A magnetic pull, an everlasting lore.

So heed the call of the vibrant night,
Let shadows guide your steps, take flight.
For in their embrace, the world shall gleam,
In specters of hope, bask in the dream.

Murmurs of the Sublime Twilight

In the hush of fading light,
Shadows dance in softest flight.
Whispers weave through twilight air,
Secrets linger, gentle, rare.

Stars awaken, shy and bright,
Casting dreams that take to flight,
Each twinkle speaks a silent tune,
Guiding hearts beneath the moon.

Colors blend in hues so deep,
Cradled in the arms of sleep.
Fragrant petals drift and sigh,
As night unfolds its velvet sky.

Ghostly echoes rise and swell,
Tales of magic, sweet and swell.
In the stillness, secrets hum,
What tomorrow may become.

With every sigh, the night invokes,
The ancient lore that softly spoke.
In the twilight's tender grasp,
Murmurs linger, hold, and clasp.

Veils of Mystique in Hallowed Glades

Amidst the trees, the shadows tread,
Veils of mystique, where dreams are fed.
Whispers of magic, softly spun,
In hallowed glades, the journey's begun.

Moonlight dances on silver streams,
Guiding the heart to wonderous dreams.
Every leaf a tale untold,
Secrets of the glades unfold.

Glimmers of hope in darkened woods,
Threaded through ancient, tender broods.
Where every sigh and fleeting glance,
Turns quiet moments into a dance.

In the heart of night, creatures stir,
Each note weaves a gentle purr.
Nature's symphony, deep and wide,
In hallowed glades, we dream and bide.

Underneath the twilight sky,
Wonders awaken, shyly shy.
The glades will hold our hopes and fears,
As time unfolds through endless years.

Flights of Phantasy in an Intangible Realm

In an intangible realm we soar,
Flights of phantasy, forevermore.
Wings of starlight brush the seams,
Carrying us on silver beams.

Veils of wonder, unseen threads,
Where every thought and dream embeds.
Worlds of wonder, bright and bold,
In every whisper, stories told.

Time dances slow as moments blend,
To the horizon where dreams transcend.
Floating free, our spirits weave,
In this realm, we dare believe.

From the depths, the visions rise,
Painting sunsets in the skies.
With each breath, new tales ignite,
In the heart of endless night.

With every beat, our dreams take flight,
In this mystical, starry night.
Where phantasy and hope align,
In realms divine, we intertwine.

The Glimmering Path of Anticipation

Upon the dawn, the path will glow,
A glimmering trail where dreams will flow.
With each step, the heart ignites,
In the soft embrace of new delights.

Hope unfurls like petals wide,
In the morning mist, our fears subside.
Every turn, a chance to see,
The beauty that is meant to be.

Sunbeams dance on dew-kissed grass,
Guiding footsteps as visions pass.
Each whisper winds through fragrant air,
Carving paths where dreams may dare.

In the silence, truth takes form,
Amidst the calm, the heart grows warm.
With every pause, the world reveals,
The depth of hope that gently heals.

Through glimmering paths, we shall roam,
In every heartbeat, find our home.
In the light of potential's grace,
We'll embrace the dreams we chase.

A Symphony of Color in the Night

Beneath the shimmering stars so bright,
A canvas unfolds in velvet night,
Whispers of hues dance in the air,
Painting the darkness with dreams laid bare.

The moon, a maestro, conducts the scene,
With silver strings and a dappled sheen,
Each shade a note in a silent song,
Where shadows and colors perfectly belong.

Crimson blooms in a garden of dreams,
Azure waves flow in soft, gentle streams,
Gold flecks chuckle in jubilant glee,
As starlight flickers, wild and free.

In twilight's magic, we find our place,
An unexpected dance, a fleeting grace,
Colors collide in a wondrous flight,
Creating a symphony in the night.

So let your heart be open and light,
Embrace the colors, lose yourself in sight,
For every moment holds beauty's embrace,
In this grand symphony, time finds its space.

Echoes of Iridescent Dreams

In the hush of twilight, dreams arise,
Whispers of color in starlit skies,
Iridescent reflections dance in streams,
Carrying echoes of our slumbered dreams.

Beneath the moon's glow, secrets unfold,
Shimmering shadows, beckoning bold,
A kaleidoscope of thoughts and wishes,
Swimming in starlight, where magic swishes.

Each fluttering dream, a fragile spark,
In the quiet night, it ignites the dark,
A tapestry woven with threads so fine,
Illuminating paths, our hearts entwined.

With every heartbeat, the night expands,
Holding our hopes in celestial hands,
Echoes of laughter mingle with sighs,
As dreams take flight, adorned with the skies.

So chase the night, let your spirit glide,
Through iridescent realms where wonders bide,
In the embrace of dreams, let us roam,
Finding our way, forever at home.

Twilight's Embrace: Revelations and Hues

In twilight's glow, the secrets unveil,
Colors entwined in a hushed, sweet tale,
A soft hand brushes against the air,
Breathing life into whispers of care.

The horizon blushes, a canvas so grand,
Each hue a promise, a silent strand,
In the fading light, revelations bloom,
Casting away shadows, dispelling gloom.

Lavender skies cradle the night,
While fireflies twinkle, sparking delight,
Every flicker, a memory recalled,
In twilight's embrace, we find hope installed.

As the stars awaken, shimmering bright,
They mirror the dreams that take flight,
With every heartbeat, a story unfolds,
In hues of twilight, our truth it beholds.

So let us cherish this magical hour,
In twilight's embrace, we find our power,
In colors and shadows, our hearts do dance,
Revelations shimmer, a wondrous chance.

Winged Secrets Beneath Enchanted Canopies

Beneath enchanted canopies, secrets lie,
Where whispers of wonder beckon the sky,
Feathers of fate flutter on softest breeze,
In the heart of the forest, a sacred tease.

The creatures of night, in shadowed suits,
Dance to a rhythm that nature roots,
With every flutter, they share their lore,
Tales of the ancients, and so much more.

Through dappled light, mysteries play,
As moonbeams entwine, leading the way,
Each leaf a story, each branch a dream,
Flowing like water, a magical stream.

With hearts wide open, we tread with care,
In the hush of the woods, we feel the air,
For winged secrets, in shadows they hide,
Waiting for whispers to be our guide.

So venture within, where enchantment thrives,
Beneath ancient boughs, our spirit arrives,
In the wonder of night, let's boldly roam,
For in nature's heart, we find our home.

Flights of Fancy in the Wearing Light

In twilight's glow, the dreams take flight,
On wings of gold, they dance through night.
Each whisper soft, a tale unfolds,
Of distant lands where magic holds.

Upon the breeze, the stories sing,
Of skies alight with shimmering things.
The stars like jewels in velvet deep,
Awake the heart and softly keep.

Amidst the shadows, hopes arise,
Like fireflies beneath the skies.
They twirl and spin, a spirited chase,
In realms where time slows its pace.

Through silver streams, the visions glide,
Where secrets of the night abide.
A tapestry of dreams unfurls,
In every thread, a world swirls.

So join the dance, let worries part,
Embrace the magic within your heart.
For in this light, our dreams take flight,
A wondrous journey through the night.

Beacons of Hope in the Whispering Shade

In shaded glades where silence reigns,
A spark of hope through darkness gains.
The whispering leaves tell tales so bold,
Of light that shines through shadows cold.

The ivy twirls in emerald embrace,
As beams of sun find their warm place.
Each ray a promise, each glint a guide,
To deeper truths where dreams abide.

Beneath the boughs, the secrets weave,
In gentle murmurs, they softly cleave.
A sanctuary where hearts revive,
In solace found, the souls can thrive.

A flicker here, a shimmer there,
With every breath, we taste the air.
Hope dances round, a fleeting muse,
In the whispering shade, we must choose.

So step with courage into the green,
Where light and shadow dance unseen.
Embrace the beacons, let them sway,
For in their glow, we find our way.

A Mosaic of Imaginative Beings

In realms where dreams and fancies twine,
A kaleidoscope of forms align.
With colors bright and spirits free,
A mosaic blooms for all to see.

The pixies flit with laughter sweet,
While ancient trees find rhythm's beat.
Each creature tells a story grand,
In every footfall, magic's hand.

From shadows deep, the wisps emerge,
With whispers soft, their voices surge.
Unseen realms where wonders gleam,
In glimmering pools of a shared dream.

The dreamers dance upon the breeze,
In swirling colors, they tease and please.
Their laughter rings through every part,
As imagination stirs the heart.

So gather round, let spirits soar,
In this mosaic, we'll explore.
For every being, both strange and bright,
Are stitched together in shared light.

Glimmers of Fantasy in Whispered Realms

In whispered realms where shadows dwell,
Glimmers of fantasy weave their spell.
The air alive with secrets old,
Stories and visions begin to unfold.

Moonlit paths invite the brave,
To chase the dreams that shadows crave.
With each soft step in silken dew,
The night reveals its hidden hue.

Creatures hidden in twilight's cloak,
Speak in riddles, their magic woke.
Through the mist, a vision glows,
A place where only the heart truly knows.

In every corner, a tale awaits,
With every turn, the magic inflates.
To touch the stars, to whisper low,
In these realms, our spirits grow.

So close your eyes and trust the sound,
Of wonder swirling all around.
In whispered realms, let magic stream,
In glimmers bright, we find our dream.

Whispers of Chiaroscuro Dreams

In twilight's embrace, shadows play,
With echoes of night, they softly sway.
Silent secrets in darkened streams,
Where moonlight stirs our hidden dreams.

Flickering lights like fireflies dance,
Inviting the heart to take a chance.
They murmur tales of forgotten lore,
In whispers that linger, asking for more.

The trees stand tall with knowing grace,
Their knotted branches, a warm embrace.
Each rustling leaf, a gentle sigh,
A lullaby sung to the starry sky.

Beneath the cloak of the silvery haze,
Mysteries woven in time's gentle maze.
Chiaroscuro, where shadows blend,
In dreams that wander, and never end.

Winged Shadows in Twilight Mist

Beneath the veil of twilight's shroud,
Winged wonders soar, both fierce and proud.
Whispers of dusk on feathered flights,
Carve stories in the softening lights.

They glide through clouds, like wraiths they roam,
In search of a place they can call home.
A symphony played by the breeze so light,
As day gives way to the velvet night.

Shadows entwined in a misty dance,
Fleeting glimpses in a tangled glance.
They flicker in the quietude air,
A reminder that magic lingers there.

As stars ignite in the darkened dome,
Winged shadows linger, lost in their poem.
In stillness, the night softly sighs,
A tapestry woven of dreams and skies.

Enchanted Creatures of the Dappled Glade

In the heart of the forest, under green light,
Creatures dwell that shimmer in sight.
With fur like silk and eyes aglow,
In the dappled glade, where wonders grow.

Beneath the canopy, laughter is free,
As fey folk spin in a jubilant spree.
Each rustle and chirp, a song so sweet,
A harmony crafted where shadows meet.

The brook hums softly, a lullaby clear,
For the enchanted beings that frolic near.
They dance with the twilight, in steps so rare,
As the moon beams down with silvery hair.

Amidst the petals and the leafy sighs,
Magic is woven where the mystery lies.
In glades of enchantment, they find their place,
In a world untouched by time's swift embrace.

Glistening Wings in a Magical Realm

In a realm where the light weaves gold,
Glistening wings of the brave unfold.
They flutter in joy with each rising sun,
Chasing the dew where the river runs.

Mystic colors paint the morning air,
With wonders that dazzle, a vibrant flare.
Each wingbeat sings of adventure bright,
In endless skies, they take their flight.

The flowers sway to the rhythm of dreams,
As laughter sparkles in shimmering beams.
In the heart of the meadow, where magic plays,
Life unfolds in a myriad of ways.

Through whispers of winds and sunlit streams,
Hope takes form in the kindest beams.
Glistening wings find their place on high,
In a magical realm, where spirits fly.

Fragments of Fantasy in the Woodland Shade

In emerald shades where secrets lay,
Whispers of magic in the leaves play.
A flicker of hope in the dappled light,
Bewitches the heart, ignites the night.

Along the path where shadows weave,
Gentle creatures, make-believe.
They dance on whispers, in playful trance,
Guardians of dreams in a hidden glance.

Mossy carpets beneath soft feet,
Each step draws closer to a world sweet.
Ancient trees leaning, secrets keep,
In silence they guard, their watch runs deep.

From trickling streams to stars above,
Nature's hug, a tale of love.
In every corner, magic thrives,
Whisp'ring softly, where wonder dives.

Return not empty from whispered glades,
For in this realm, no fear pervades.
Hold these fragments close to your heart,
In woodland shade, we'll never part.

A Symphony of Color in the Dimness

Amid the twilight, colors blend,
A symphony where shadows mend.
Each hue whispers a tale untold,
A canvas of wonders, both brave and bold.

Emerald greens and sapphire dreams,
A tapestry woven with moonlit beams.
In the soft glow, the world takes flight,
Where every petal dances in light.

Golden rays kiss the dusky ground,
Painting moments where joy is found.
Crimson skies in a fleeting embrace,
A heartbeat echoing time and space.

In the fading light, serenity plays,
With vibrant echoes of sunlit days.
The night wraps 'round like a tender sigh,
Beneath the stars, let our spirits fly.

So gather the colors, hold them tight,
In the dimness, they spark delight.
For every shade that the night may borrow,
Holds hues of laughter and dreams to follow.

Wandering Spirits in a Vibrant Abyss

In the vibrant depths where echoes roam,
Wandering spirits find their home.
From shadow and light, they weave and dart,
In the night's embrace, they play their part.

With laughter that dances on the wind,
They whisper secrets of worlds unpinned.
A symphony of souls in the twilight glow,
In every heart, their stories flow.

Shattered dreams and memories bright,
Echo in hues of the secret night.
Through swirling fog and shimmering mist,
Each spirit treads, a fleeting twist.

In every shadow, a story lingers,
Touched by the chill of ancient fingers.
For in the abyss where colors bleed,
Life finds solace, and hearts take heed.

So heed the call from the depths unknown,
For within the vibrant, spirits have grown.
In the wandering night, together we'll tread,
On paths where mysteries are lovingly spread.

Shimmers of Light Embracing the Dark

In the midnight hour, shimmers gleam,
A dance of light, a silvery dream.
Embracing the dark with gentle grace,
Filling the void of this sacred space.

Stars like candles flicker and sway,
Guiding lost souls along the way.
In shadows, they quietly weave a thread,
Of hope and whispers, where angels tread.

Every glimmer tells a tale old,
Of battles fought, and courage bold.
With every breath, the night hums low,
Carrying secrets only the brave know.

So fear not the dark when the day is done,
For light blossoms where shadows run.
Let shimmers guide you through the night,
To find your dreams in the soft twilight.

Together we'll gather the stars above,
Crafting a symphony of light and love.
In every heart, a beacon shall spark,
As shimmers of hope embrace the dark.

Fantasies Weaved in a Forest of Flying Lights

In a forest glimmering bright,
Where fireflies dance in the night,
Whispers of magic take flight,
Dreams unfurl with sheer delight.

Gossamer threads of the unknown,
Weave tales where ancient seeds are sown,
Every leaf a secret shown,
In this realm, we feel at home.

Stars peek through the verdant sky,
Painting visions that never die,
In the glow of a lullaby,
Hearts will soar, they long to fly.

Roots entwined with stories old,
In the silence, legends told,
In this space, pure joy unfolds,
Mysteries wrapped in marigold.

So come, dear wanderer, and see,
Where wonder blooms, wild and free,
Under the shade of the grand tree,
Forever lost in fantasy.

Secret Gardens of Imagination's Flight

Beyond the gate where no paths tread,
A garden waits with dreams unspread,
Where thoughts take root, where wishes bred,
In petals soft, sweet stories fed.

Lilies whisper secrets rare,
Amidst the fragrance, magic's flair,
With every breeze, we lift our care,
In a place where hearts lay bare.

Vines entwine with a gentle grace,
In their embrace, we find our place,
Colors swirl, a wondrous space,
In the silence, find our pace.

Butterflies dance on golden beams,
Weaving through our gentle dreams,
In the laughter, the sunlight gleams,
A tapestry of fleeting themes.

So let us wander, hand in hand,
Through these gardens, so unplanned,
Where imagination can expand,
And hearts unite, a soft command.

Kaleidoscope Reveries in an Elven Glade

In the glade where the colors collide,
Magic flows like a gentle tide,
Reflecting worlds where dreams abide,
In every shadow, secrets hide.

Wondrous echoes of laughter ring,
As delicate wings begin to sing,
Underneath the joy they bring,
Life's sweet dance, eternal spring.

Sparkling waters weave through the trees,
Whispers caress in the tender breeze,
A realm that bends, a mind to tease,
In every moment, pure heart's ease.

Crickets play their symphonic tune,
Guiding wanderers 'neath the moon,
Every heartbeat a soft boon,
In this wonder, we are strewn.

So come, dear dreamers of the night,
In this elven realm, take flight,
Through a kaleidoscope of light,
Embrace the magic, pure delight.

Ethereal Textures of Wanderlust's Whisper

Beneath the skies of twilight's hue,
Whispers beckon, calling you,
From corners rare that few pursue,
In this realm, the heart breaks through.

With every step, the world unfolds,
Tales of wonder, rich and bold,
In shimmering sights, we are consoled,
As pathways weave in threads of gold.

Ethereal winds of time do sigh,
Carrying dreams that soar and fly,
Every moment, a soft goodbye,
In wanderlust's embrace, we lie.

The echoes of distant lands call clear,
In the silence, we draw near,
With each heartbeat, shedding fear,
In this journey, we revere.

So wander forth, the world is vast,
In textures rich, our dreams are cast,
With every breath, embrace the past,
In whispers of wonder, we're steadfast.

The Allure of Celestial Gardens

In gardens where the twilight glows,
The stars above weave tales of old.
Each flower holds a secret dream,
And silken petals whisper bold.

Moonlit paths, where shadows dance,
Invite the heart to wander free.
In fragrant air, enchantments prance,
Among the blooms, a symphony.

The fragrance of forgotten lore,
In gentle breezes softly hums.
With every step, the spirit soars,
To find the magic that it drums.

Illuminated skies above,
Glow with the dance of fireflies.
Hearts find solace, hearts find love,
In gardens where the night draws nigh.

A tapestry in velvet night,
Holds secrets that the stars might tell.
In every bloom, a spark of light,
The allure of gardens, cast a spell.

Daydreams in the Whispering Woods

In woods where ancient whispers play,
The sunlight spills on emerald leaves.
Each step unveils a world at bay,
Enticing hearts to weave and thieve.

Beneath the boughs, the dreams take flight,
As laughter echoes, soft and clear.
With every glance, a new delight,
Awakens wonders, ever near.

Misty mornings call the lost,
To tread where time and dreams entwine.
Among the trees, no soul's a cost,
Each heart finds solace, pure and fine.

A symphony of nature sings,
As breezes dance through woven trails.
In every rustle, magic clings,
To tales of old and whispered gales.

The woods hold secrets meant for two,
In daydreams shared, we linger long.
Lost in the shade, where shadows grew,
We find our place, where we belong.

Twilight's Tapestry of Winged Wonders

In twilight's hush, the colors blend,
The sky adorned in hues of gold.
With each soft flutter, joys extend,
And nature's stories, bright and bold.

The wings of night unfurl with grace,
As fireflies weave a dance divine.
In every corner, find your space,
Where dreams take flight and stars align.

Hidden among the velvet dark,
Are whispers of a magic flight.
Each creature sings a tiny spark,
Of stories shared in fading light.

In splendor's grasp, the heart complies,
To catch the vision, swift and sly.
In every beat, the wonder flies,
A tapestry beneath the sky.

Oh, winged wonders, come and play,
In twilight's embrace, we'll find our way.
To weave our dreams in shades of night,
And dance with joy, till dawn's first light.

Secret Lives of the Nightly Garden

When night descends on quiet lands,
The garden wakes with murmurs sweet.
Each shadowed corner, magic stands,
Where dreams and silence softly meet.

Among the blooms, the moonlight spills,
Illuminating hidden sights.
The garden pulses, laughs, and thrills,
With secrets held through starry nights.

Petals close, but hearts expand,
In whispered tales of love and life.
Each creature stirs, its stories planned,
In joyous moments free from strife.

In twilight's glow, the world transforms,
As magic cloaks the gentle earth.
In every sigh, a wonder warms,
The nightly garden's quiet birth.

Oh, secrets held in dreams untold,
In every fragrance, history unfolds.
The secrets thrive, the stories blend,
In nightly gardens, time transcends.

Hues of Magic in a Timeless Realm

In a realm where shadows gently play,
Colors dance in a soft ballet.
Crimson whispers, azure gleams,
Casting spells through waking dreams.

Through ancient woods where secrets lie,
Emerald leaves reach for the sky.
Golden sunlight, a tender kiss,
In this magic, we find our bliss.

Mystic rivers, uncharted streams,
Reflecting all our wildest dreams.
With every twist, a story told,
In hues of magic, brave and bold.

The moonlight weaves its silver lace,
In every corner, time and space.
A tapestry of stars above,
Whispers of forgotten love.

In twilight's glow, the world ignites,
With every heart, the magic lights.
Together we shall take our flight,
In hues of magic, pure delight.

Dances of Light in the Secret Orchard

In an orchard hidden from the day,
Where sunlight twirls in bright array.
Petals shimmer, the breeze a sigh,
As secrets waltz and shadows fly.

Golden apples, ripe with dreams,
Reflecting laughter in silver beams.
Under the boughs where visions dance,
Whispers of life in a sweet romance.

Crickets chirp their midnight song,
For in this space, we all belong.
With every step, the world unfolds,
In dances of light, our hearts consoled.

Luminous nights and twilight's charms,
Inviting us to seek new arms.
Where fireflies weave their glowing threads,
In every corner, adventure spreads.

In the secret dusk, we find our way,
Beneath the stars, our hopes at play.
Together we dream in fragrant air,
In dances of light, we shall declare.

The Ethereal Canvas of Nature

Upon the canvas, nature paints,
With strokes of kindness, love, and saints.
Mountains rise with strength profound,
While rivers dance with a joyful sound.

The golden dawn, a blazing sphere,
Whispers secrets only we hear.
With every hue, a gentle touch,
A world of beauty, oh so much.

Beneath the stars, the cosmos calls,
In moonlit shadows, wonder falls.
Each flower blooms, a story spun,
In the tapestry of everyone.

The breeze carries tales of old,
Of forgotten days and dreams untold.
Each heartbeat syncs with nature's song,
In harmony, we all belong.

In this ethereal realm, we roam,
With every step, we find our home.
In nature's arms, let magic rise,
On this canvas, the heart complies.

Enigmatic Flights of Fancy

In the twilight, we take to air,
With dreams unfurling, light as a prayer.
On enchanting winds, our spirits soar,
Through realms unknown, forever more.

Whispers of adventure fill the night,
As shadows twist in playful flight.
With every shadow and glimmering star,
The heart knows well just where we are.

In the hush of twilight, secrets glide,
With every thought, the universe wide.
Illusions fleeting, truths entwined,
In enigmatic beauty, we find.

We chase the echoes of dreams untold,
With wings of gossamer, brave and bold.
In the depths of night, we shall embrace,
This dance of fancy, this boundless space.

With every heartbeat, new paths to tread,
In the enchanting dusk, we'll be led.
Together we fly, forever free,
In enigmatic flights, just you and me.

Prism Dreams in the Heart of Twilight

When twilight drapes the world in blue,
A prism glimmers, dreams break through.
Whispers of magic fill the air,
As shadows dance without a care.

Glimmers of hope in fading light,
Sparkle like stars, precious and bright.
In each heartbeat, a story pure,
A tapestry of dreams, secure.

Through emerald woods, the secrets twine,
With every step, they intertwine.
In the hush of dusk, we find our way,
To chase the dreams that softly sway.

A tapestry spun with threads of night,
Where every color catches light.
Here in the heart, the wonders gleam,
In the magical twilight's dream.

As stars awaken from their sleep,
We gather memories, ours to keep.
In the glow of a luminous sphere,
The prism dreams, both far and near.

Celestial Luminaries in a Dream-Touched Wood

In the wood where dreams take flight,
Celestial luminaries ignite the night.
Twinkling lights among the trees,
Whisper secrets in the breeze.

Moonbeams dance on silver streams,
Illuminating hushed, sweet dreams.
Every shadow holds a tale,
In this enchanted, moonlit vale.

Starlit blossoms, petals in bloom,
Brighten the path, dispelling gloom.
Each glimmer casts a spell so grand,
In this magical, dream-strewn land.

Crickets sing a lullaby,
As nocturnal whispers softly sigh.
The world fades in a gentle glow,
As the heart learns the night's sweet flow.

Together we tread on a silver beam,
In a wood wrapped in a dream-like theme.
Celestial luminaries guide our way,
As night unfolds a magic play.

Hidden Wonders Beneath the Celestial Canopy

Underneath the starry vault,
Hidden wonders, pulsing, fault.
Each twinkling star a glowing key,
Unlocks the whispers of the sea.

The moon hangs low, a watchful eye,
As secrets weave where shadows lie.
In silken air, the night unveils,
The hidden paths of winding trails.

Beneath the sky, a magical dance,
Every silent moment, a chance.
In the depth of night, dreams swirl and dive,
And all the hidden wonders thrive.

With starlit fingers, the night bestows,
A tapestry where magic flows.
Wrapped in sighs, the heart will soar,
Chasing wonder, forevermore.

In quiet corners where shadows meet,
Mysteries linger, bittersweet.
Underneath this celestial dome,
Wonders whisper, beckoning home.

Spectral Silhouettes Dancing in the Night

Spectral silhouettes twirl and glide,
In the depths where dreams abide.
With every flicker of starlit beams,
Reality melts, giving way to dreams.

Through the veil, the shadows play,
Dancing softly, night turns to day.
In their rhythm, we find our grace,
A magical waltz in time and space.

Glimmers of laughter weave through air,
With every step, we shed our care.
Together we sway, lost in delight,
In this moment, shining bright.

The moonlight watchers, wise and true,
Guide the way for me and you.
In spectral forms, we find our song,
A heartbeat shared, where we belong.

With every twirl, the shadows gleam,
We lose ourselves in this soft dream.
Spectral silhouettes, come join the night,
As we dance under stars, our hearts take flight.

Whispers of Color in the Gloaming

The twilight whispers secrets rare,
In hues of gold and softest air.
A canvas painted by the night,
Where dreams and shadows blend in flight.

The trees adorned in amber glow,
As gentle breezes start to flow.
With every rustle, tales unwind,
Of magic that we seek but find.

Beneath the stars, the petals sigh,
A serenade to the evening sky.
Each color speaks in muted tones,
A symphony of whispered moans.

In this enchanted, tranquil space,
The world transforms, a wondrous place.
Where every heart can feel the spark,
Of mysteries hidden in the dark.

Luminescent Beings and Enchanted Terrain

In glades where fairies dance and twine,
Their laughter echoed, bright as wine.
With wings that shimmer, soft and light,
They weave through branches, pure delight.

The soil beneath, a river's gleam,
Reflecting life, a silver dream.
Each flower blooms with secrets deep,
In twilight realms where wonders sleep.

The animals, with eyes aglow,
Lead wanderers through paths of woe.
For in the woods, where magic brews,
Each heart finds joy, each soul renews.

A guardian spirit, bold and fair,
Protects the lands with tender care.
Through tangled vines and whispered lore,
They bridge the gap to ancient score.

A Silken Journey Through a Magical Realm

On silken threads that glisten bright,
We weave our way through dreams at night.
Each step a whisper, soft and rare,
In lands where magic fills the air.

Through corridors of woven light,
We travel far, beyond our sight.
With every turn, enchantments grow,
A world unseen, yet deeply known.

The rivers hum a mystic tune,
As stars align with the crescent moon.
In fragrant fields where wishes flow,
A tapestry of dreams we sew.

With laughter echoing on the breeze,
We chase the shadows, hearts at ease.
In every glance, a treasure found,
In every echo, magic's sound.

The Allure of Fantastical Beings at Dusk

As day yields softly to the night,
The wondrous creatures take their flight.
With eyes like gems and laughter sweet,
They gather 'round where mysteries meet.

With hidden paths of velvet glow,
They dance in circles, swift and slow.
Each being holds a hundred tales,
Of starlit quests and distant trails.

Their voices blend in harmonies,
A song that stirs the wildest trees.
In twilight's grasp, they weave their lore,
Of ages past and legends more.

As dusk unfolds its velvet shroud,
The magical, they sing aloud.
For in this hour, dreams take flight,
And hearts unite in pure delight.

Ethereal Creatures of the Moonlit Grove

In shadows deep where whispers play,
The moonlit grove begins to sway.
With creatures strange, both shy and bold,
Their stories in the night unfold.

A spirit fox with eyes aglow,
Dances where the starlight flows.
With feathered wings, the nightingale,
Sings softly as the shadows pale.

Mysterious lights like fireflies,
Twirl and twinkle in the skies.
Each flicker tells a tale unique,
Of magic found in dreams we seek.

The trees stand tall with secrets deep,
Guarding promises they keep.
In every branch, a fable lies,
Awaiting for the night to rise.

As dawn approaches, creatures flee,
Into the depths of mystery.
Yet echoes linger, soft and sweet,
A melody where shadows meet.

Celestial Dances on Gossamer Threads

Beneath the stars, on silver lines,
The universe in balance shines.
Mystic beings take their chance,
To waltz in rare celestial dance.

With threads of light, they weave and spin,
Creating worlds, where dreams begin.
The nightingale, with voice so pure,
Calls forth the spirits to endure.

Across the sky like shooting stars,
They twine their fates with radiant scars.
Gossamer ties, so frail yet strong,
Bind them together, where they belong.

In cosmic halls, where echoes sing,
The dance of time takes vibrant wing.
Every twirl an ancient rhyme,
A beat that stitches generations' time.

The moon looks down, a watchful guide,
As secrets in the cosmos bide.
With every trail of starlit thread,
A tapestry of dreams is bred.

The Painted Veil of Dreaming Creatures

In realms where colors blend and sigh,
The painted veil drapes low and high.
Creatures of dream flicker near,
With eyes that hold both hope and fear.

A rabbit spun of twilight's hue,
Leaps through a field of morning dew.
Its coat a swirl of night and day,
In vibrant strokes, it bounds away.

The fox, an artist with its brush,
Colors the world with a gentle hush.
Each pawprint leaves a mark of light,
A fleeting whisper in the night.

Across the veil, a dragon flies,
With wings like waves of painted skies.
It breathes a dream in every flight,
A canvas stretched beyond the night.

Through wonderous fields, the creatures chase,
The colors blend, a soft embrace.
In their playful dance, we find our voice,
In the painted veil, we all rejoice.

Mysteries in the Misty Moonlight

In moonlight's cloak, the world is blurred,
With secrets whispered, seldom heard.
As mist weaves through the ancient trees,
It carries scents of mysteries.

A silhouette steps lightly forth,
Drawing shadows from the north.
With silver hair and eyes of deep,
It gathers whispers, while we sleep.

The owls take flight, a watchful crew,
Illuminating paths anew.
Their silent wings, like velvet night,
Guard truths that shun the morning light.

In silent corners, wonders lie,
Wrapped in moonbeams, low and high.
A leaf may rustle, a branch may creak,
Echoes of stories that dare not speak.

Yet, listen close, the night reveals,
The grandeur that the starlight steals.
In misty glades where shadows twine,
The heart of magic starts to shine.

Rainbow Phantoms in a Twilight Garden

In twilight's glow, the colors seep,
Where shadows linger, secrets keep.
A whispering breeze, soft and light,
Guides the dreams that take their flight.

With petals bright like jewels rare,
They dance aloft in evening air.
A tapestry of hues unfolds,
Each thread a memory that it holds.

The stars above begin to gleam,
In the garden's heart, a delicate dream.
Where phantom forms in silence play,
Their laughter echoes, then slips away.

Beneath the arch of velvet skies,
The twilight blooms, where magic lies.
In every corner, stories hum,
Of love and loss, where shadows come.

As dawn approaches, colors fade,
Yet in our hearts, the dreams are laid.
Rainbow phantoms, bright and bold,
Remain as whispers, tales retold.

Fluttering Tales Beyond the Veil

Beyond the veil, where shadows leap,
Whispers flutter, secrets keep.
In twilight's hush, the stories glide,
On wings of magic, dreams abide.

A brook sings soft, a gentle tune,
As fireflies wink beneath the moon.
Each flicker tells of worlds anew,
Of fluttering tales known by few.

In hidden nooks, the echoes play,
Of laughter lost in yesterday.
A tapestry of whispers spun,
Reveals the truths we thought were done.

With every breeze, a tale takes wing,
A hundred voices start to sing.
Beyond the veil, where shadows weave,
The tales of old still interleave.

In the quiet dawn, the stories bloom,
Dispelling night, dissolving gloom.
Fluttering tales, like leaves in flight,
Guide lost hearts towards the light.

Secret Whispers Beneath the Starlit Canopy

Beneath the stars, a hush descends,
Where nature speaks and silence mends.
In every rustle, secrets dwell,
In whispered breaths, the night will tell.

The moonlight spills on silver streams,
Awakening forgotten dreams.
A melody of twinkling light,
Guides the wanderers of the night.

Each star a beacon, bright and true,
Holding stories known to few.
In shadows deep, the echoes stir,
Of ancient tales that softly blur.

The canopy, a cloth so vast,
Stitches our futures with the past.
In the stillness, thoughts entwine,
Secret whispers, so divine.

As dawn approaches, secrets fade,
Yet in our hearts, their mark is laid.
Beneath the stars, we find our way,
In quiet whispers, lost in sway.

The Dance of Colorful Illusions

In the realm where colors gleam,
Illusions swirl, as if in dream.
With every step, they intertwine,
The dance of shadows, line by line.

A painter's brush, with strokes so bold,
Creates a story yet untold.
Each hue a heartbeat, lost or found,
In whispers soft, they swirl around.

The moments flicker, bright and brief,
Like autumn leaves that twist in grief.
A symphony of vibrant sights,
Unfolds beneath the starry nights.

In every twirl, the past collides,
Where memories and dreams abide.
The dance of fate, a vivid play,
Illusions lead us on our way.

When morning breaks, the colors wane,
Yet in our souls, they still remain.
In every heartbeat, every glance,
We cherish still this vibrant dance.

Enchanted Echoes of Nature Unbound

Whispers of leaves in the gentle air,
A melody sung by creatures rare.
In shadows deep where the moonlight plays,
Nature's canvas in soft, silver ways.

A brook that babbles with secrets untold,
Rivers of stories in waters bold.
Dancing fireflies weave in the night,
Guiding the hearts with their flickering light.

Mountains rising like ancient dreams,
Wrapped in the mist, or so it seems.
The echoes of time through the valleys flow,
A symphony felt, though whispers are slow.

Blossoms of colors, as bright as the sun,
Painting the fields, where wildflowers run.
The world spins softly on nature's breath,
Each moment cherished, defying death.

In stillness found by a woodland sigh,
Magic seeps through, as spirits fly.
Each note a promise, a wondrous sound,
In enchanted echoes, we're forever bound.

The Colorful Cadence of Fabled Nights

Stars awaken in a twilight glow,
They whisper secrets that none may know.
In blankets of night, with colors alight,
Dreams dance on edges of starlit flight.

Fables entwined in the songs of the breeze,
Where shadows and light find a way to tease.
A chorus of wonders, the nightingale's call,
Painting adventures that beckon us all.

Moonbeams weave tapestries, shimmering bright,
Stitching together the dreams of the night.
With echoes of laughter from those we adore,
The cadence of color, we endlessly explore.

Each heartbeat a story, a world yet to see,
In hues of enchantment, we dance wild and free.
So gather your wishes, let starlight ignite,
The colorful cadence of fabled nights.

As dawn approaches with a soft, rosy hue,
The magic fades slowly, but lingers anew.
In the heart of the dreamer, the colors will stay,
Alive in our spirits, come night or come day.

Twilight Tales in a Mythical Wonderland

Beyond the veil where the shadows play,
Whispers of magic lead our way.
In twilight tales, where legends awake,
A mythical journey, each step we take.

Silvered streams sing to the trees,
Carrying echoes on the evening breeze.
Creatures from stories leap into view,
A whimsical dance in the soft twilight hue.

Glimmers of hope in the fading light,
As stars begin to sparkle, bright.
With wishes sown like seeds on the ground,
In this wonderland, pure joy is found.

A tapestry woven with threads of the past,
Every stitch a memory, meant to last.
Hold tight to the tales that the shadows reveal,
In twilight's embrace, all wonders are real.

As dusk flows softly into night's domain,
Imagine the magic as dreams break the chain.
For in every heart, in the stillness, we find,
A mythical wonderland, forever entwined.

Veils of Color in a Forgotten Realm

In a land where time drifts like a fragile sigh,
Veils of color sweep beneath the sky.
Hidden away in the whispers of noon,
A forgotten realm, where shadows croon.

Ruby and gold paint the edges of fate,
Twisted and tangled, as if by a fate.
Each petal that falls tells a story anew,
Of memories lost, and of hopes that grew.

Cascading laughter through the trees rustles,
The magic of moments, like delicate bustles.
In echoes forgotten, we search for the light,
In veils of color, all dreams take flight.

A lantern of hope flickers softly inside,
Illuminating paths that no longer hide.
Bring forth the courage, and dance in the glen,
For in this realm, we begin once again.

In this tapestry of shadow and hue,
The forgotten find solace, the lost find their due.
A world that revitalizes dreams that once seemed,
In veils of color, we dare to be redeemed.

www.ingramcontent.com/pod-product-compliance
Ingram Content Group UK Ltd.
Pitfield, Milton Keynes, MK11 3LW, UK
UKHW050357230125
4239UKWH00074B/192

9 781805 631545